A Note to Parents

DK READERS is a compelling program for beginning readers, designed in conjunction with leading literacy experts, including Dr. Linda Gambrell, Distinguished Professor of Education at Clemson University. Dr. Gambrell has served as President of the National Reading Conference, the College Reading Association, and the International Reading Association.

Beautiful illustrations and superb full-color photographs combine with engaging, easy-to-read stories to offer a fresh approach to each subject in the series. Each DK READER is guaranteed to capture a child's interest while developing his or her reading skills, general knowledge, and love of reading.

The five levels of DK READERS are aimed at different reading abilities, enabling you to choose the books that are exactly right for your child:

Pre-level 1: Learning to read
Level 1: Beginning to read
Level 2: Beginning to read alone
Level 3: Reading alone
Level 4: Proficient readers

The "normal" age at which a child begins to read can be anywhere from three to eight years old. Adult participation through the lower levels is very helpful for providing encouragement, discussing storylines, and sounding out unfamiliar words.

No matter which level you select, you can be sure that you are helping your child learn to read, then read to learn!

DK

LONDON, NEW YORK, MUNICH,
MELBOURNE, and DELHI

Editorial Assistant Ruth Amos
Senior Editor Hannah Dolan
Designer Toby Truphet
Jacket Designer Rhys Thomas
Pre-Production Producer Rebecca Fallowfield
Producer Danielle Smith
Managing Editor Laura Gilbert
Design Manager Maxine Pedliham
Art Director Ron Stobbart
Publishing Manager Julie Ferris
Publishing Director Simon Beecroft

Reading Consultant
Linda B. Gambrell, Ph.D.

Lucasfilm
Executive Editor J. W. Rinzler
Art Director Troy Alders
Keeper of the Holocron Leland Chee
Director of Publishing Carol Roeder

Rovio
Approvals Editor Nita Ukkonen
Senior Graphic Designer Jan Schulte-Tigges
Publishing and Licensing Manager
Laura Nevanlinna
Vice President of Book Publishing
Sanna Lukander

First published in the United States in 2013 by
DK Publishing
345 Hudson Street, New York, New York 10014
10 9 8 7 6 5 4 3 2 1
001-196557-Nov/13

Page design copyright © 2013 Dorling Kindersley Limited

Angry Birds™ & © 2009–2013 Rovio Entertainment Ltd.
All Rights Reserved.

© 2013 Lucasfilm Ltd. & ™. All rights reserved.
Used under authorization.

DK books are available at special discounts when purchased in bulk
for sales promotions, premiums, fund-raising, or educational use.
For details, contact:
DK Publishing Special Markets
345 Hudson Street, New York, New York 10014
SpecialSales@dk.com

A catalog record for this book is available
from the Library of Congress.

ISBN: 978-1-4654-1539-4 (Paperback)
ISBN: 978-1-4654-1540-0 (Hardcover)

Color reproduction by Altaimage, UK
Printed and bound in China by L-Rex

Discover more at
www.dk.com
www.starwars.com

Contents

DK **READERS**

ANGRY BIRDS
STAR WARS
II

PATH TO THE PORK SIDE

Written by Scarlett O'Hara

Band of birds

Meet the good guys
in a galaxy of greedy pigs!
Don't tell anyone, but
their leader, Yoda Bird,
is hiding a mysterious Egg.
If the evil pigs find The Egg,
it will give them great power.

Peckmé
Amidala

Quail-Gon

Yoda Bird

Sneaky pig

R2-EGG2

C-3PYOLK

Obi-Wan Kaboomi

Redkin Skywalker

Moa Windu

The birds might not all be as good as they seem. Could one of them be about to turn to the Pork Side?

Talent spotted

Many years ago, two respected birds named Quail-Gon and Obi-Wan Kaboomi visited a planet called Tatooine. There, they discovered a special young bird named Redkin.

Quail-Gon and Obi-Wan Kaboomi wanted Redkin to become a Jedi Bird like them. They wanted Redkin to help fight the horrible pigs, but first he needed a little training.

Jedi Birds

The Jedi are a group of wise warriors. They study an energy called the Force, which helps make them powerful.

Podracing
suit

Life on Tatooine

Young Redkin Skywalker
grew up on Tatooine.
His favorite hobby was podracing.
Redkin even built his own
super-fast podracer!

Redkin also built a droid bird called C-3PYOLK. C-3PYOLK is a helpful servant droid. He has very good manners.

Scrap metal body

Podracing helmet
Podracing is a dangerous sport, so Redkin wears a protective pilot helmet with goggles.

Jedi training

Redkin is now a Jedi Padawan. Obi-Wan Kaboomi is the Jedi Master who is training Redkin. Redkin can be a difficult student, but Obi-Wan has lots of patience.

Padawan hair braid

Padawan
A bird who is in training to become a Jedi Bird is called a Padawan.

Redkin often gets into trouble. He is impatient to know everything about The Egg. He thinks Obi-Wan isn't telling him everything about it.

Long Jedi hair

Queen Bird

Peckmé is Queen of Naboo. The evil hogs want to attack her because she is on the birds' side. They can't hurt her, though. Not when her protector and pilot Captain Namaka is around!

Pig-scaring blaster

Can you keep a secret?
Redkin has a crush on Peckmé.
Peckmé secretly knows this but
most of the time she likes to
pretend not to notice him!

Admiring
glance

Beauty
spot

Darth
Swindle

Count
Dodo

Darth
Moar

Meet the Pigs

Watch out for the nasty pigs!
They include sneaky Darth
Swindle, evil Count Dodo,
wicked Darth Moar, the stupid
Copypigs, mean General
Grunter, and the silly battle pigs.

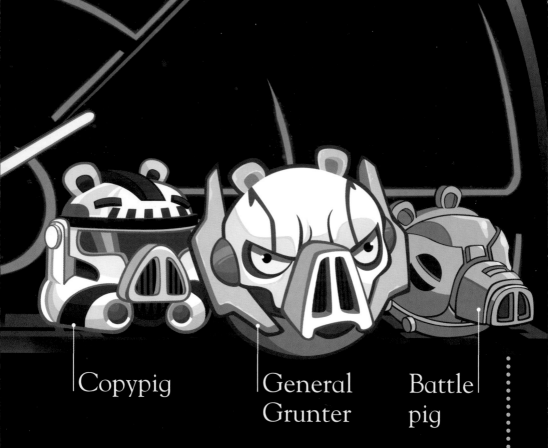

Copypig

General
Grunter

Battle
pig

The pigs all want to get
their hooves on The Egg.
They have heard about a
talented bird called Redkin.
They want him to join their
side so he can help them find
The Egg.

Lightsaber

Swine surveillance

Be careful! General Grunter
is a very mean Pig Lord.
He would do anything to please
his Master, Darth Swindle.
He has an army of battle pigs.
Grunter orders them to spy on
the young Jedi Bird Redkin.

General Grunter tells Swindle
all about Redkin, so that the
Pig Lord can tempt Redkin
to the Pork Side.

Shiny
metal

Battle pigs
These pig-like robots,
or droids, are programmed to
follow orders for the Pork Side.

Lovebirds

Don't tell anyone, but Redkin
and Peckmé have fallen in love.
Only R2-EGG2, C-3PYOLK—
and now you—know about it.

Peckmé sees only the good
side of Redkin Skywalker.
She could never imagine that
he would turn to the Pork Side.
Will he prove her wrong?

Piggy plotting

Darth Swindle plans how to tempt Redkin to the Pork Side. He pretends to be nice and becomes friends with Redkin.

The Force

Swindle is kind to Redkin.
He tells him that he is very smart
and lets him taste junk food.
He tells him that together
they can find the powerful Egg.
Redkin is very tempted by
Swindle's sneaky snortings.

Jedi
robes

Good egg gone bad

Redkin feels torn.
He loves Peckmé and feels
loyal to the Jedi Birds.
However, he thinks his feathered
friends might be keeping secrets
about The Egg from him.

Jedi
utility belt

Redkin gobbles up the junk food Darth Swindle gives him. He is desperate to find The Egg. His whole appearance changes. Is he already on the Pork Side?

Scary yellow eyes

Angry beak

Birds in a flutter

Almost nothing gets past the wise Jedi Master Yoda Bird. Yoda Bird knows Redkin could fly off to join the Pork Side. Yoda and Moa ask Obi-Wan to find Redkin and stop him.

Obi-Wan agrees to the mission. Can he save Redkin from the power of the Pork Side?

Jedi
Padawans

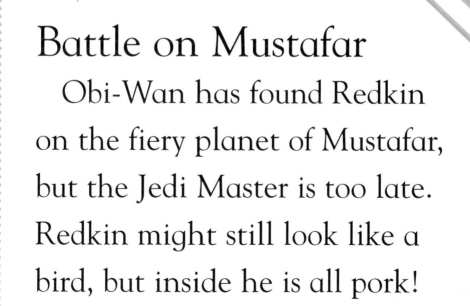

Battle on Mustafar

Obi-Wan has found Redkin
on the fiery planet of Mustafar,
but the Jedi Master is too late.
Redkin might still look like a
bird, but inside he is all pork!

Obi-Wan asks Redkin to
turn back to the birds' side,
but Redkin won't change.
Look out! Feathers fly as
Redkin and Obi-Wan have
a fierce lightsaber duel.

Lard Vader

You might not realize it,
but you have met Lard Vader
before. It is Redkin!
He is now the terrible Pig Lord
Lard Vader.

Obi-Wan beat
Redkin in their duel
on Mustafar.
Redkin escaped, but
he was badly injured.
Now Redkin has to wear a
special helmet with a pig-like
snout to help him to breathe.

Pig apprentice Redkin is no longer a Jedi Bird. He has become Darth Swindle's greedy pig apprentice.

Redkin Skywalker's path to the Pork Side is complete.

Where is The Egg?

Those spiteful pigs might have a new recruit, but they still don't have The Egg! Only Yoda Bird knows where The Egg is hidden. Can you guess where The Egg might be? It has a "cracking" disguise.

The Egg
The Egg is filled with a powerful energy called the Force. Whoever finds it will have the power to rule the galaxy.

It is disguised as the droid
bird R2-EGG2!
For now, at least, the secret
is safe…

Quiz

1. Who built the servant droid C-3PYOLK?

2. Peckmé is queen of which planet?

3. Who else knows that Peckmé and Redkin have fallen in love?

4. Where does Obi-Wan duel with Redkin?

5. Why does Lard Vader wear a special helmet?

1. Redkin Skywalker 2. Naboo 3. R2-EGG2 and C-3PYOLK
4. Mustafar 5. To help him breathe